BOOK FIVE

WOWbook

Guest Editor
Lynda Monk

5

Welcome to WOWbook 5

BOOK FIVE

Welcome to another exciting edition of WOWbook. We have a plethora of talented artists sharing their techniques, and we know there will be something to interest everyone in this issue.

Alice Fox shows us how to make botanical inks from leaves, plants and vegetable matter – I can't wait to have a go at making my own. Mary McIntosh uses bleach and discharge paste to create her stunning pieces, and Jenny O'Leary demonstrates a quicker and more accessible process for the technique of batik. I'm so looking forward to trying out these two workshops. Holly Hart creates sketches of animals and plants found in the UK to create her stitched hangings, while Melanie Missin transfer dyes a design from old net curtains. Maggie has interviewed Jean Draper, which gives us an in-depth look into Jean's background and how she works. Our 'Inspired by' series continues with the letter C: from Coventry Cathedral to the coast, it's always interesting to find out what inspires artists to produce such wonderful pieces of work.

I could certainly do with some inspiration at this moment. Having recently moved from the edge of a small town in Essex to a quiet little village in Lincolnshire, it has taken me some time to settle in. No sirens, no traffic and none of the noise generally associated with town living. All I can hear are the birds singing and the occasional tractor.

There is much to be done and, of course, my workroom was first on the list. I'm pleased to say it is now finished and it's so good to have one large space instead of two smaller rooms. The best part for me was unpacking everything and sorting through. I found several things I had forgotten about so my 'must do' list has now grown considerably. All my toys are out and ready to be played with. My storage boxes are also sorted and labelled and the room has been

^ Jenny O'Leary, *Welsh Trees*. Batik on tissue.

arranged so that one end is the messy space, the other end is for sewing and everything else is in the middle. The only problem is that it is so tidy – very unusual for me – which is why I need to be inspired to get in there and create. With *WOWbook 05* in my hand, I have no excuse!

We would be really interested to know where you do your creative work. Do you have your own dedicated room or do you work on the dining table or in the kitchen? Maybe you share a room.

Let us know on our members-only Facebook page and perhaps share a photograph with us.

Lynda Monk

> Mary McIntosh, *The Tipsy Stitcher*. Piece based on the traditional Drunkard's Path design.

INK MASTER
Making and using botanical inks

∧ Potential mark-making tools.

Alice Fox

What are botanical inks?

Ink is basically a coloured liquid that can be used to draw, write, print or make marks on paper. In this case we are using plants (leaves, flowers or vegetable matter) to give the liquid colour. In many ways it is just one step beyond a dye but would generally be more intense in colour and the addition of a binder will help the liquid sit well on the paper. Ideally, our coloured liquid will be of a suitable consistency to write or draw with a dip pen, but if we think laterally it could be used with any other mark-making tool. Making your own botanical inks is quite experimental, so why not also be experimental with how you use them?

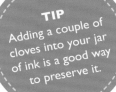

TIP
Adding a couple of cloves into your jar of ink is a good way to preserve it.

< Sketchbook drawings in botanical ink (using tea and iron).

> Text and drawn marks in botanical inks (using elderberry and alum, and walnut).

∨ A selection of botanical inks in re-used bottles and jars.

Longer-lasting colour

Making your own inks with home-grown, foraged materials, or those readily available in the kitchen, can be a spontaneous way of making your own coloured art materials. If you are making inks for immediate use, you don't need to worry about preservatives but there are ways of keeping these inks for longer-term use. Vinegar and salt (added during cooking), alcohol (added after cooking) or even just popping a couple of cloves into your jar of ink are all ways to make sure your inks don't go mouldy or smelly.

Once you understand the basics of botanical ink-making there are all sorts of possibilities that you might try. Some plants are better than others at producing colour and as you experiment you will learn which work well and which might not be worth a second attempt. I undertook lots of experiments as part of my MA research, using plants from my allotment plot. I tried all sorts of things, some of which I wouldn't bother with again, but others produced surprisingly interesting results.

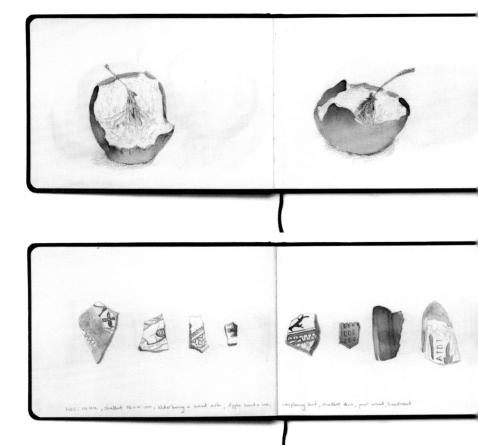

∧ Sketchbook pencil drawings (top) of apples made using botanical ink (holly wood).

∧ Sketchbook pencil drawings (bottom) of ceramic fragments made using botanical inks.

< Sketchbook page showing the alkaline effect of viola flower ink on acid-free paper.

TIP
It is safe to make ink in your kitchen, but just make sure you keep all utensils separate from those used for preparing food.

Importance of pH

Some plant-based inks are sensitive to pH acidity, others less so. All plant material is acidic to a certain extent. If we add vinegar to the recipe (as a preservative) this will make our ink more acidic and can affect the colour. Most art papers are acid free. If it doesn't say 'acid free' on the packet, then you can assume it is slightly acidic. If your paper is acid free this means that it is likely have an alkaline effect on your ink. For some inks this will have no effect, but for others there will be a change, either as soon as you apply your ink to the paper, or over time as the ink dries and the pH shifts. It's worth being aware of this possibility to explain shifts in colour on the page compared with the ink in your jar.

To make your ink alkaline (for some plants this will have an effect) you can use bicarbonate of soda. Iron can also be used to shift the colour of some inks. This generally darkens or 'saddens' (a traditional term from natural dyeing) the colour. Including iron in your recipe could have a slightly corrosive effect (we're talking over a very long term here). Traditionally ink was made using oak galls and iron and there are many historical documents that exist intact with such ink. Adding gum arabic as a binder is not necessary but can help the consistency of your ink, make it flow better from a dip pen and help it sit on the surface of the paper. Gum arabic can be bought in powdered form or as a liquid from art suppliers.

Some botanical inks will be more colour stable than others and some may fade more quickly than others. Many commercial art materials and dyes will also fade in daylight, so natural isn't necessarily any less permanent. This process isn't always about predictability – but let's have an adventure!

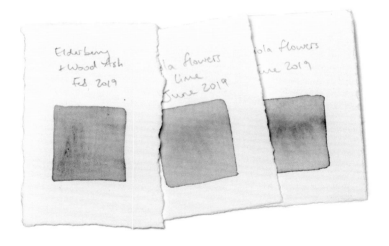

∧ Recording botanical ink colours on paper as a reference.

Recipe for ink using onion skins

I'm using onion skins in this example, which is a good place to start. Save your onion skins in the kitchen each time you use one: they keep well in a paper or cloth bag. You can use yellow skins or red ones, getting different colours from each.

∧ Dried onion skins used to make botanical ink.

MATERIALS AND EQUIPMENT

- Stove
- Stainless steel pan or bowl
- Sieve or strainer
- Onion skins
- Vinegar
- Salt
- Bicarbonate of soda
- Iron water (see page 9)
- Stirring stick (re-use a wooden lolly stick or coffee stirrer)
- Paper for testing
- Funnel
- Coffee filters
- Clean jars or bottles
- Labels
- Gum arabic (optional)

∨ Sketchbook drawing of onion skin in botanical ink made with dried onion skins.

How to make red onion ink

1. Break up the onion skins with your hands into small fragments.

2. Put the broken skins into a stainless steel (or other non-reactive) pan or bowl.

3. Cover with water and bring slowly to a simmer.

4. Cook gently for around 30 minutes or until the liquid looks dark with colour.

5. Strain off the skins and compost these, squeezing them to extract the precious coloured liquid.

6. Continue to cook the liquid slowly to concentrate the colour but don't let it boil dry. Keep testing the colour on paper as you go.

7. Divide the liquid between two clean jars to make different colours.

8. Mix half a teaspoon of bicarbonate of soda with a similar amount of water (adding more liquid at this stage will dilute the colour, so keep this to a minimum). Add this to one jar to make ink number one.

9. Add a teaspoon or two of 'iron water' to the other jar, or alternatively add a couple of rusty nails or washers to the jar and leave for a day or so for the iron to affect the ink.

10. You can strain your inks further at this stage using a coffee filter and a funnel.

11. If you are adding gum arabic as a binder, do this as the last stage.

∧ Found rusty objects.

< 'Iron water' in a jar.

∨ Iron water used on scrapbook paper.

Making 'iron water'

1. Put some rusty objects in a jar. Fill it up with about one-third to one-quarter vinegar and then top up with water. Leave without a lid in a well-ventilated area and away from food and children, for example in a shed or cellar.

2. Each day pour the liquid into another container (leaving the iron objects behind) and then later on (or the next day) pour it back into the jar with the iron. This gets oxygen into the process and helps the iron to make more rust.

3. Repeat this on a daily basis. After a week or two the water will be turning orange and can be used in small amounts to add iron to inks.

4. Keep the jar topped up with the water-and-vinegar mix as you use it.

5. Keep the clearly labelled jar in a safe place away from food preparation and children.

Taking it further

Other plant material to try

Buddleia is one of those plants that pops up all over the place, so even if you don't have a garden there is probably some growing on wasteland not far away. Whether you have permission to pick in a garden or you gather flowers from the wild, make sure to take only a small amount, leaving plenty for the insects that love this shrub. If you don't want to use the flowers straight away, you can dry them and store for use at any time of year. You can get a green ink from the fresh flowers (with alkaline) and yellows through to caramel browns from dried flowers. Many flowers are sensitive to pH so this ink may well shift as you apply it to paper.

Viola flowers soaked in water will release a beautiful purple pigment, which can be reduced down to the right consistency for use. As are many flowers, this is sensitive to pH, so it might be rich purple in the jar, turning to a stunning turquoise on acid-free paper. Try drying the flowers as they are ready to pick so that you build up enough to use.

Beetroot (chopped and cooked) will give you an intense bright pink, especially with vinegar added. However, the colour will be 'fugitive', meaning it will slowly fade to brown.

Some berries will also give you instant bright colours, which may not stay stable over time, but are fun to play with. Freeze them first to burst the cells and then defrost, crush in a pestle and mortar and strain off the juice, which becomes your ink. Adding bicarbonate of soda to the berry juice will shift the colour from pink tones to blues or greys.

Walnut ink is another traditional botanical ink, using the fleshy green husks surrounding the nut shell. It produces a beautiful rich brown ink that can be darkened with iron and has natural anti-fungal properties, so it doesn't need a preservative. Be warned – it stains whatever it touches, which is why it's such a good source of ink. Be careful, therefore, not to let it boil over while you cook it up. Simmer the fleshy green husks for a couple of hours, strain then continue to simmer to reduce to a suitable consistency.

∧ Dried buddleia flowers.

> Recording botanical ink colours on paper as a reference.

< Botanical ink made from dried tagetes flowers and alum. Ink was applied to the paper using a feather. Dried tagetes flowers.

I can't wait to see your experiments with botanical inks – don't forget to share your work in our members-only Facebook group or on our blog.

FURTHER READING

Botanical Inks: Plant-to-Print Dyes, Techniques and Projects by Babs Behan, 2018. ISBN 978-1-7871315-6-9

Natural Processes in Textile Art: From Rust Dyeing to Found Objects by Alice Fox, 2015. ISBN 978-18499429-8-0

Make Ink: A Forager's Guide to Natural Inkmaking by Jason Logan, 2018. ISBN 978-1-4197324-3-0

The Organic Artist: Make Your Own Paint, Paper, Pigments, Prints and More from Nature by Nick Neddo, 2015. ISBN 978-15925392-6-0

FLYING HIGH
Painted and machine-stitched birds

Holly Hart

MATERIALS AND EQUIPMENT

- Resource images
- A selection of papers including handmade paper
- Pencil
- Inks
- Paintbrush
- Calico fabric
- Water-soluble fabric
- Medium-weight interfacing
- Natural-coloured wools or fabric scraps
- Pins
- Sewing machine
- Embroidery foot or darning foot
- Cottons and metallic threads (suitable for machine embroidery)

Getting started

Before starting a large project, I always like to make a quick initial sketch to see how the composition might work out. I use this as a rough guide throughout the whole making process.

I collect vintage wildlife books from which I get much of my resource material. I also collect many other resource materials such as photographs, magazine pictures, stamps, etc. and keep these in my sketchbooks along with my own quick sketches and drawings.

< *In Flight*. Finished piece with close-up of goldfinches in flight.

< I use vintage flora and fauna books for my resource material.

> A quick initial sketch is made to see how the composition works. This will be used as a rough guide throughout the making process.

I tend to stick to drawing plants and animals found in the UK. Sometimes, when my books don't quite get me thinking, I pop outside to get some inspiration.

Gather your resource materials together and make a basic sketch of how you would like your final piece to look. You might choose to look through books or even take a little walk – something may just inspire you.

< A selection of my sketchbook pages.

Sketching on the fabric

I begin by concentrating on the main feature of my piece – in this case, the goldfinches.

1. Use a pencil to sketch onto the calico fabric. I enjoy using calico as a base instead of paper because I think the pencil and ink sits better on the fabric. Calico also lends itself to being stitched onto.

When it comes to the flowers and plants, I like to use a variety of papers as well as calico. Brown paper, handmade paper and greaseproof paper all work well.

2. Once all the pencil outlines have been drawn, it's time to start using ink. Work over your initial pencil lines with a fine paintbrush and black ink. At this stage, you can start to create shading by using ink washes for darker areas. Don't feel the need to make all your lines solid – broken lines can add a delicate touch to a piece.

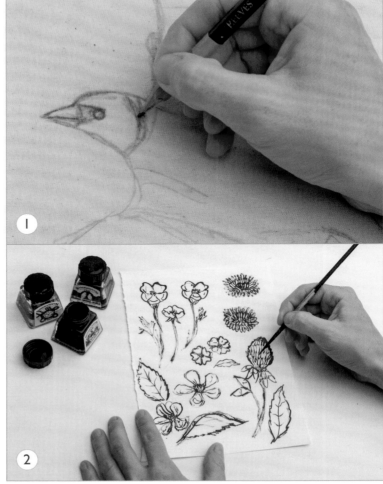

< Brown paper and handmade paper have been used for the initial pencil sketch before working over the lines with black ink.

3. Once all the black ink and washes are dry, you can start on the colour. Be as bold or as subtle with your colour as you like. I like to leave some of the plants and flowers as they are, with just the black and light washes. I tend to leave metallic inks and any white highlights to the end. Be patient with layering colours: wait for your ink to dry to avoid any muddy puddles forming on the fabric. Remember, you can always add more colour but it can be very difficult to remove it!

4. When you have finished adding colour or shading and the pieces are totally dry, carefully cut around the edges of the larger shapes. You may wish to leave some of the smaller shapes in place until the next stage.

< Pencil sketch on calico outlined with black ink before adding washes of colour.

∧ This coloured bird has been cut out and is ready to be stitched to the background.

∧ I have outlined my bird in black ink before colouring it, and it is now ready to be cut out.

The stitching process

Now all your pieces are ready, you can begin the stitching process.

1. Attach medium-weight interfacing to the back of all the pieces to give them stability. It's a good idea to pin the interfacing in place as it can move while stitching.

2. If you have a darning or embroidery foot, use this on your machine as it gives you much more movement to play with. Go over your initial black ink lines with the sewing machine, building up layers of stitch as you go. You can add lots of layers of stitch or keep it simple. For more textured areas, such as fur or fluffy feathers, overlapping layers of stitch helps to create the natural texture.

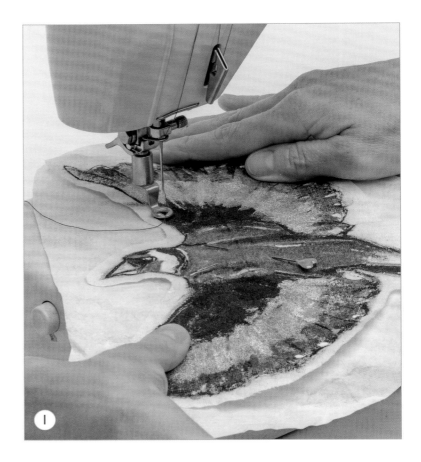

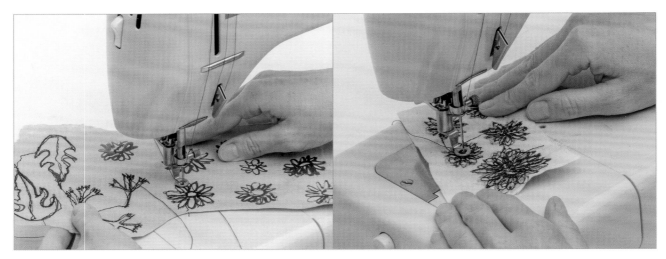

∧ Free machine embroidery is used on the brown paper shapes following the inked lines.

∧ These flower shapes, drawn on calico, have been outlined with free machine embroidery using a black thread to make them really stand out.

Moss and undergrowth

Now that we are at the sewing machine, this is a great time to start making our moss or undergrowth.

1. Take your water-soluble fabric and cut it into strips, around 6in long and 2in wide (15 x 5cm).

2. Layer pieces of natural-coloured wool or fabric on top of the water-soluble strip.

3. When you are happy with the arrangement, you can stitch over the top. Repeatedly sew on top of these pieces to keep them in place.

4. Make sure to fill the strips of water-soluble fabric with overlapping stitches. I used gold thread for this with white thread on the bobbin, but you could use any colour you wanted. Soft greens and earthy browns would work well to create a more realistic moss.

5. Once you feel your strip is full of stitches, you can dissolve the water-soluble fabric. Place the strip under a tap or into a bowl of warm water. Rub the fabric gently with your fingers to make sure you dissolve the entire fabric strip. It is important that you don't have any loose lines of stitches as they will fall apart once the fabric is dissolved. Set aside the remaining stitched piece until it is dry. Repeat this process with all your strips.

> Make a little nest or a hidey-hole from the machine-stitched strips.

< I like to make lots of strips at a time so I always have some ready in my stash.

Finishing off

Now it's time for placement. Get all your pieces together and lay them next to your chosen background. Handmade paper is a brilliant choice for a base background. Why not try and make your own paper to make your piece of work extra special?

< Lay the stitched pieces onto your chosen background. Re-arrange the pieces until you are happy with the layout.

I look forward to seeing your wildlife pictures and hope you will share your work in the WOWbook members-only Facebook group.

∧ *Mr Badger*. Drawn and painted with machine-stitched flowers.

< *In Flight*. Finished piece using mixed media, onion paper, calico, inks, paper, machine embroidery.

I tend to frame my larger creatures with plants and other smaller animals, so they go down first. It might take a couple of re-arrangements until you are happy with your composition. If you can't quite decide which arrangement you prefer, then it's a good idea to take digital photographs of several different arrangements, which you can then view before your final decision.

When you're happy with your arrangement, machine stitch the pieces in place.

Feel free to draw back into the piece with inks or paint once everything is attached.

Taking it further

You could use any animal or bird as your inspiration. *Mr Badger* was made after I spotted one snuffling around in my garden one evening. I have drawn and painted this piece, adding machine-stitched flowers, and finally framing with a basic wooden picture frame.

INSPIRED BY...
COASTLINE
with *Sheila Warner*

I love walking and spend a lot of time outdoors, exploring the coastline of the United Kingdom. The jagged rock formations of Cornwall's coast have always inspired me and, in the past, I have created textile art based on this area. Recently, whilst walking along the east coast, I was taken by the open marshland and have been inspired to reproduce the various grasses and seascapes of the region – not a craggy rock in sight!

Blakeney saltmarsh in Norfolk is where the inspiration was found for this particular piece – the skeleton of an old fishing boat, left to decay, showing a broken structure which I thought would be a challenge to stitch. I set my mind to how to recreate those textures of the decaying ribs and the flaking paint of the boat, against areas of moss and marshland. Many photographs were taken and sketches drawn to refer back to once I got home.

Back in my studio, I studied my numerous photographs and sketches. I looked at the way the grasses moved with many shades of one colour and how this area merged into the sea; how the soft mossy area is a completely different texture. There was a puddle on the land where the boat had been left, which produced a diverse element to be created without the use of glitzy material or threads. The rotting wood and crumbling paint also needed to be considered, along with the foreground of the boggy area. All these different views and textures were a test of my ability to achieve my interpretation of the open coastline.

I always work on artist's canvas because all my pieces are heavily machine stitched and artist's canvas will not stretch, tear or distort. A frame or stabiliser is not required as the canvas is stiff enough to work on alone. Daler Rowney Artist acrylic paints are used, as I feel they give a better finish than student-quality paints, and also Inktense pencils which, when dry, produce a permanent ink effect.

The boat was the main feature in this piece, so getting that right – the size, proportion and texture – was of paramount importance. Taking a small sample of canvas and having the boat picture next to my Bernina sewing machine, I free machine stitched a portion of the hull to see how I could create the boat. Using acrylics and Inktense pencils on the wet canvas, colour was applied to develop the boat's paintwork and rotting wood. Many samples were produced to create different textures for the various areas of the picture. Notes about the mix of paints and threads used were made as I went along.

Once happy with my samples, I started work on the main piece, machine stitching the outline of the boat, the horizon and various areas within the picture. Once the outline sketch had been stitched, I wet and then painted the canvas. The machine-stitched lines kept the colours in place, stopping them from spreading.

When the work was completely dry, it was time to start free machine stitching the many components of the piece, referring constantly to my samples and photos and using many different shades of thread and many layers of stitch. If you lose focus, it is very easy to over-stitch a piece. In this case, if more stitching had been added to the boggy area or the puddle, the boat would not have stood proud. Less is definitely more!

I am a member of the 02 Textiles Group – you can find out more about my work here:
www.02textiles.co.uk/SheilaWarner.html

∧ *Coast.* Inspired when walking along the Norfolk coast. My initial sketch and painting (page 20) and my finished piece (above) using a combination of painting and freehand machine embroidery on artist's canvas.

∨ *Penda Banner II* was made using woad-dyed wool flannel which was screen-printed with boar drawings. Pagan symbols were painted on with oil pastel and the piece was then hand stitched using linen thread.

> *Lichen Micro.* For this piece I used hand-dyed noil silk, with painted pigment-adjusted puff binder. It was then needle-felted with alpaca wool and extensively hand stitched.

Colour is an essential part of my creative practice, not only for the aesthetic but to communicate its psychological meanings. The 'Colour Affects' system I follow combines colour harmony with the science of psychology, and I apply its principles to my creative work, my colour consultancy and across my life. It means my colour palettes are harmonious and communicate something specific: a feeling, a personality, psychological traits.

Typically, my colours are warm and usually tertiary. They can take longer to create as they come from much over-dyeing or over-printing/painting. In this process, I find my colour wheel invaluable – if only to double-check my instincts on how to achieve a specific colour. It is worth the extra effort as rich and unusual colours are often the result.

Usually I dye my background cloth and then select the threads, fibres and pigments within my chosen colour palette. Sometimes I prefer a tonal palette, where hues are a slight variation of each other, creating something subtle. On other occasions I prefer a more contrasted palette, with colours creating a more vibrant combination – it just depends on what I am trying to say. The fibres used are usually selected, pre-dyed, but I tend to individually mix my print and painting pigments unless I find something pre-coloured that fits my palette. This may all seem rather laborious but to me, it's an important part of my creative practice, and if the colours are not right, the piece just isn't right either.

The pieces shown here demonstrate different uses of colour. The green piece *Lichen Micro* is on noil silk and to get this particular background colour I did lots of sampling. I settled on this yellowy-green colour – not too dark and oppressive, but lighter and brighter to give a more optimistic feeling. The puff binder colour was also carefully tested to find the right balance of medium and pigment to achieve a colour that blended in. Marled alpaca wool was needle-felted, and both tonal and contrast coloured threads were hand stitched to give the depth of a rich forest floor.

The blue piece *Penda Banner II* is part of a collection made for a project with twenty-nine other artists, called 'Face to Face', at ArtistsWorkhouse, Studley. Our theme was Penda, an Anglo-Saxon pagan king of Mercia. Captured by the idea that Penda was always at war, my collection focused around his army's standards and banners.

As I imagined King Penda rallying his troops and encouraging them to follow him into battle, I chose blue as the colour of communication. I hand dyed wool flannel in woad and painted and screen-printed boar imagery and crude pagan symbols in soft complementary colours, including a kingly old gold. Linen threads were then hand stitched in contrasting colours for extra detail and texture. The lighter colours on the dark blue background suggest they have faded into the cloth, giving a sense of an old banner that was carried into battle by Penda and his army – or so I imagined!

More of my work can be seen on my websites: *www.mariaboyle.co.uk* and *www.mariaboylecolour.com*

INSPIRED BY...
COLOUR
with *Isobel Moore*

Ever since I can remember, I've had a touch of synaesthesia – meaning that I see some concepts (such as days of the week) as colours. For example, Tuesday is yellow and Thursday is navy blue. Like many teenagers, I went through a phase of just wearing black. My grandmother was determined to break me out of it and to my horror, she knitted me a shocking-pink fluffy jumper for Christmas. I refused to wear it but pink is now one of my favourite colours! In my first teaching job, I had a very strict headteacher who banned the use of black paper for displaying children's work. All the teachers had a secret stash at the back of the cupboard, as sometimes black is exactly what you need to make other colours pop.

I learned colour theory through City & Guilds, and I remember things my mother used to say, such as 'blue and green must never be seen' rattling around in my head. But learning to use colour in my embroidery has come from experience, time, and experimenting. Some of my first pieces of City & Guilds work were pretty dreadful because I was trying too hard to use the theory learned in class; I've found that trusting yourself always works better. Creating art is a process of making decisions, and those decisions are based on our experiences, our preferences, and all the different things that make us unique individuals. There are always tips and tricks to using colour that we can pick up, but the only way to create really unique art is to trust yourself and get stuck in. When I'm teaching, I love how the same idea can look completely different across a group of people, largely because of the colour choices they have made.

I buy nearly all my materials in charity shops; initially this was for financial reasons, but it's now also an ethical choice. Sometimes I buy things to chop up but I end up wearing them! I pick things out for the colour first, then the pattern. I wash and trim new finds, keeping any colourful buttons in a jar and adding the fabric pieces to my stash. As such, my palette is organic, ever changing and growing, and unique to me. I use the tiniest scrap and when I've finished a piece of work, I tend to start the next one using the scraps that are left on my desk. This imposes a natural limit and can spark more creativity than having an endless choice.

< *Summer Garden*. This piece was made using embroidered and embellished handmade felt with the intention of cutting it up to make circles – I thought it was a cunning plan to make more work in less time (I'm currently working to a deadline for an exhibition). However, there was an outcry on my Facebook page when I mentioned 'scissors', so it remains intact. I have since added hand stitching and beads.

I have recently started to play with paint to generate ideas as I love the immediacy. Embroidery, even fast machine embroidery, can be quite slow to achieve results. This has prompted me to start making felt again (something that I learned years ago, before machine embroidery) and I've dusted off my embellisher to add my favourite fabric and thread scraps. Using an embellisher to add colour with fibres and fabrics is very much like painting – it's just as quick, and it's pure joy to play around with colour and achieve immediate results. Handmade felt is wonderful to stitch into. I've combined my new-found love of embellishing colourful handmade felt with my love of curves and circles to create the three pieces shown here.

You can see more of my latest experiments on my website: **www.isobelmoore.co.uk**

> *Garden at Sundown* (top right) and *Tree of Life* (bottom left). These two pieces are made from handmade felt with machine embroidery. I love stitching into felt and wanted to experiment with circular design ideas.

INSPIRED BY...
COUNTRYSIDE AND COASTLINE
with *Libby Smith*

Having lived in north Essex for most of my life, I've spent many hours walking the country tracks, ancient pathways and estuarine coastline of East Anglia. With its characteristic undulating farmland – rich in history as well as agriculture – abutting pretty villages with thatched cottages, windmills, watermills and centuries-old churches, there is much to discover and explore. Whether walking from Great Bardfield to Finchingfield, Wickham St Paul to the Maplesteads, both Little and Great, Clare to Hundon and Poslingford or along the Tollesbury saltmarshes, I always return home with my pockets full of treasures, such as conkers, feathers, bits of rusty metal and wool gathered from the fences and thorny hedges along the way.

I use my camera when I'm out, as I'm not good at making quick sketches, and find it easier to capture on camera what I see – the texture, the light, and the effects of weather on that particular day. Once home, I look at the marks, shapes, colours and textures before sampling some of these in my sketchbook. I tend not to aim for an accurate depiction of a landscape but more an impression or composition of what I recall.

∧ *Tollesbury Saltmarshes*. Inspired by the Essex coast at the mouth of the River Blackwater, Tollesbury Wick and the RSPB (Royal Society for the Protection of Birds) Manor Farm Nature Reserves; and by the sound of grasses rustling in the breeze, the sun sparkling on the water, the pink-grey mud and rotting timbers. Sheep and cattle graze freely with no fences to be seen, looking across to Mersea on one side and Bradwell on the other.

I start by making marks on natural fabrics such as silk organza, mousseline, lightweight habotai, silk net and cotton scrim, using a combination of cold water, fibre-reactive dyes with a thickener to give me a wider range of effects, and acrylic paints for the finer marks. Having more control over the dye, I can prevent the fabric from being completely flooded with colour, as I find the element of white or quieter tones is very important. It's the subtle shading and nuances of colour that attract and excite me. When I'm happy with my palette of fabrics, I start to collage, layer, reposition and pin until the composition starts to come together. This can be a lengthy process and I may need to walk away from it for several days and look at it again with fresh eyes. I like the fabric to inform me as to what I'm seeing: the colours peeping through might indicate a distant field, watery channels or shallow mudflats and rotting timbers. Hand stitching is added to secure and add further detail and texture.

Once the piece is finished, I try to explore different ways of mounting my work and recently I've taken to visiting a salvage yard in Colchester where I found some old wood panelling – easier to handle and lighter than floorboards. Once I've selected a piece, it's reduced to the appropriate length, loose paint and splinters are removed, and a damp cloth is used to take away any dirt. The piece of work is then stretched lengthwise, leaving the top and bottom edges to reveal the wood.

You can find out more about my work on the EAST (East Anglian Stitch Textiles): *www.easttextile.co.uk*

∨ Images from my sketchbook. I like to get something down on paper quickly. This may not be a true reflection of a particular place but an impression of what I have seen.

∧ November Landscape was made for the EAST exhibition entitled 'Between the Lines' commemorating the end of the First World War.

INSPIRED BY...

COVENTRY CATHEDRAL

with *Ann Cooke*

In 2013, I paid a visit to Coventry Cathedral, looking for inspiration to help me create a new body of work for an upcoming exhibition – and inspiration is certainly what I found!

The Cathedral was awash with colour along each side of the nave and from the baptistry window it looked stunning – but then the large west window came into view. This window is plain glass etched with saints and angels through which you can see the ruins of the old church.

The work shown here was part of an exhibition with the textile group 'Connected' using Coventry Cathedral as the inspiration. The exhibition was displayed in various locations across the UK.

∧ *The Baptistry Window I.* Solid blocks of colour were produced using a variety of stitches, threads and beads on black muslin, mounted on a background of coarse linen/cotton slub fabric.

> *The Baptistry Window II.* To create this piece, the stitches I used included satin stitch worked in different directions, split and chain stitches, needle-weaving, couching, French knots, bullion knots and stem stitch.

The baptistry window

My work is based on the baptistry window which is a large piece and radiates colour from the centre outwards, graduated from clear through yellow, greens, blues, reds and gold. When you view the window closely, it is the design within each panel that creates the graduation.

The fabrics used in my pieces are not graduated but are actually solid blocks of colour. I worked with a variety of stitches and threads to interpret the design, which is stitched on black muslin and mounted on a background of coarse linen/cotton slub fabric.

To produce *The Baptistry Window* I used matt and shiny silks, metallics, cottons and variegated synthetic threads with various sizes of round and bugle beads, some of which I dyed myself. Metallic fabric formed the background. The stitches include satin stitch worked in different directions, split and chain stitches, needle-weaving, couching, French and bullion knots and stem stitch.

The west window

The pieces shown here replicate part of the west window. The images were produced using free machine embroidery on organza. I drew the images on water-soluble fabric, laid the organza on top and then fitted it tightly into an embroidery hoop. With a mixture of excitement and apprehension, I lowered the feed dogs on my machine and began sewing, slowly at first but, after a while, managing to pick up speed. When all the sewing was completed, I released the fabric from the hoop and gently ran water over the piece to dissolve the water-soluble fabric. When dry, I placed the work on a ceramic tile, heated up the soldering iron and carefully went around the edges of the stitched image.

< *St Columba Carrying a Dove*. St Columba (c.521–597) was a missionary from Ireland who founded the community on the island of Iona in Scotland. This piece was produced using free machine embroidery on organza.

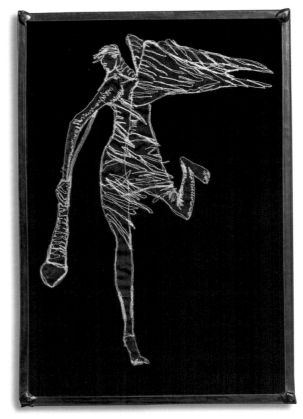

< *Angel I*. I loved the thought that the angels were having a party, playing music and kicking their heels. The design was first drawn on water-soluble fabric, then organza was placed over the top and free machine embroidery worked over the outlines.

LIFE'S A BLEACH!
Creating layered designs

Mary McIntosh

In this workshop we will be using Jacquard Decolourant and household bleach to remove colour from black fabric, creating layered designs.

Any coloured fabric can be used but the results are most dramatic on black. Black fabrics vary and although most of them will work very well with bleach, not every black will discharge successfully. Always do a sample test first.

MATERIALS AND EQUIPMENT

- Black cotton or linen fabric
- Plastic table covering
- Padded surface – an old sheet or large towel or a drop cloth over a padded board
- Pins
- Jacquard Decolourant
- Thick household bleach
- Old plate or saucer
- Freezer paper
- Craft knife and cutting board
- Sponge brush/sponge roller
- Small paintbrush
- Stamps, rubbing boards, stencils
- Old steam iron
- Protective gloves and apron
- Face mask – FPP3 or full respiratory mask recommended

> Discharge paste and household bleach have been applied through stencils onto black cotton to create this stunning wallhanging.

Setting up your work station

Cover your work table with a plastic sheet and place your padded board or surface on top. Pin the black cloth to the padded surface around the edge.

Stage 1
Using Jacquard Decolourant

The first process in this technique is to remove some of the colour from the fabric with Jacquard Decolourant, using freezer-paper stencils.

1. Using the craft knife and cutting board, cut out shapes from freezer paper. I used circles here and cut around various sizes of cups, saucers and plates. Any shape, or combination of shapes, could be used. Keep the cut-out shapes and put to one side for now. To create a more ragged, organic look, tear your stencils or use torn masking tape to mark out areas.

2. Iron the freezer-paper stencils onto your fabric using a dry iron. The freezer paper will temporarily adhere to the surface. Make sure you place the freezer paper shiny side down onto the fabric and just peel off when you have finished.

3. Pour some Jacquard Decolourant onto an old plate or saucer.

4. Use mark-making and patterning methods to apply the decolourant to the area inside each stencil.

Why not try...

- Use a small paintbrush or sponge brush to 'draw' a design.
- Use the sponge brush to liberally apply decolourant onto a stamp block. Press down firmly onto the fabric, using a rocking motion to get a really good print. Any stamps can be used including commercial stamps, wooden blocks, homemade stamps from funky foam, lino, rubbers, etc. You could also try corks, bottle tops, sponge dabbers – anything you have to hand – for making marks.
- Use rubbing boards in the same way as stamp blocks. These could be commercial rubbing boards or your own rubbing boards made from textured wallpaper glued to card and given a protective coating or PVA glue or varnish. Apply the decolourant in the same manner as you did for the stamp blocks.
- Stencils work well with this technique. Lay the stencil on top of the freezer-paper cut-out and apply the decolourant with a sponge brush or sponge roller.
- Try mark-making with an old credit card to create lines across the freezer-paper aperture. Apply the decolourant to the edge of the card using a sponge brush. Experiment with other mark-making tools.

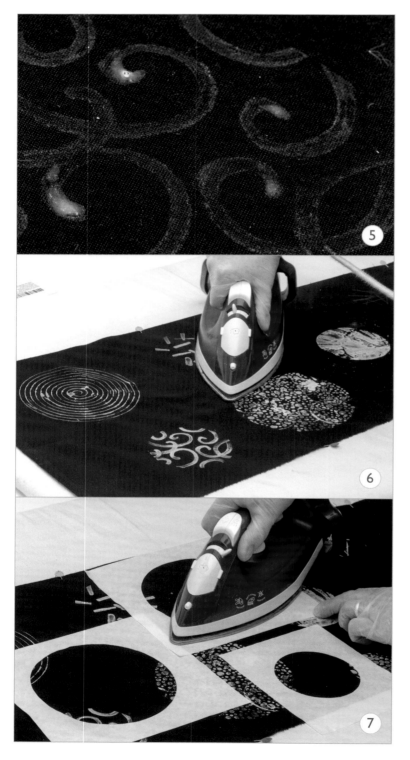

5. Allow the decolourant to dry. It will become almost transparent. Make sure it is totally dry before steam ironing.

6. Add water to your iron, set on a high heat setting and turn on the steam. Slowly iron the areas of decolourant to remove the colour and reveal your design. The stencilled areas of decolourant slowly change appearance as you iron them. Keep ironing until you are satisfied that the decolourant has been fully activated.

7. Return to the freezer-paper stencils and reposition on the ironed fabric, overlapping some of the areas with the colour previously removed with decolourant, and iron into place with a dry iron, ready for the next stage.

Stage 2
Using household bleach

Applying bleach to the fabric gives the work more depth. The bleached areas appear to sit behind the decolourant sections.

1. Pour a little bleach into an old saucer and place close to your work to prevent dripping.

2. Using any or all of the marking and patterning methods suggested above, apply the bleach through the freezer-paper stencils.

3. Use the bleach sparingly. This will start to work almost immediately it hits the fabric, so you need to work quickly.

4. Iron immediately to prevent the bleach from spreading. As you iron, the bleached design will deepen in colour. Remember to wear your face mask and avoid the bleach fumes.

5. The bleach will appear to be behind areas of decolourant and give the work more depth.

You can continue to reposition your freezer-paper stencils and work with both decolourant and bleach up and down your fabric to create overlapping and layered designs.

WARNING
Beware the 'bleach drip'. Bleach is not as thick as decolourant, so move your saucer near to the area you are working on to avoid leaving a bleach trail or drip.

> Bleach has been applied sparingly to a rubbing plate using a sponge brush, then ironed immediately to prevent the bleach from bleeding out.

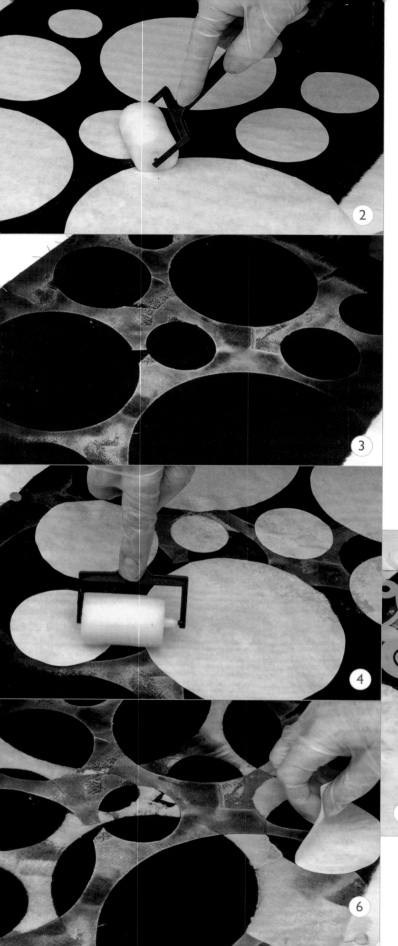

Positive and negative grid designs

You can also use the shapes cut out from the freezer paper – the 'holes' – to create a negative design.

1. Place your freezer-paper shapes onto the fabric, leaving a small gap in between, and iron in place.

2. Using a sponge brush or sponge roller, apply decolourant over the top. Keep unpeeling and repositioning your shapes as you move down the cloth.

3. Allow the decolourant to dry, remove the freezer-paper shapes, and use a steam iron to remove the colour.

4. Replace the freezer-paper shapes, overlapping some areas of decolourant, but still keeping some areas black, and repeat using household bleach. Remember to iron as you go to stop the bleach from spreading too quickly. The result looks as though the bleach grid sits behind the decolourant grid, creating depth – it's magic!

5. As an alternative, use a stencil laid over your negative shapes to create a lacy grid.

6. Try combining the positive shapes and negative grid designs.

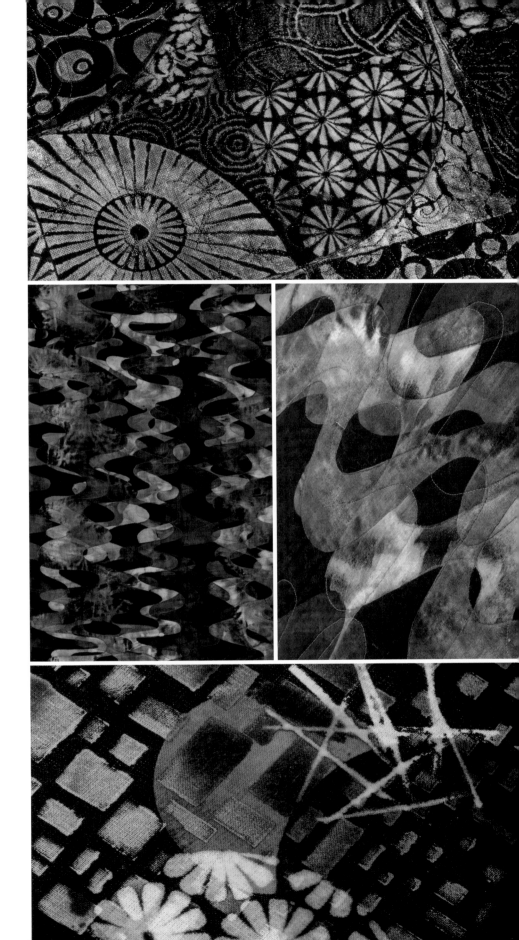

> *The Tipsy Stitcher.* This piece is based on a traditional Drunkard's Path quilting block. Decolourant and bleach were used to create the pattern.

Taking it further

- Cut freezer-paper shapes that tessellate and butt these up to form a design – like this piece on the right which was based on a traditional Drunkard's Path block, but using decolourant and bleach to create the pattern. My version is called *The Tipsy Stitcher.* You could also try squares, rectangles and hexagons.

- Mix in some coloured pigment to the decolourant to add colour as well as removing it. The piece *Ebb and Flow* uses Dynaflow mixed in with the decolourant (50/50 mix) to give the greenish tones.

- Screen-printing inks or fabric paints mixed with decolourant will sit on the surface of the cloth giving yet another layer of depth.

> *Ebb and Flow.* Dynaflow has been mixed with the decolourant to add colour as well as removing it.

> Fabric paints mixed with decolourant sit on the surface of the cloth, giving yet another layer of depth.

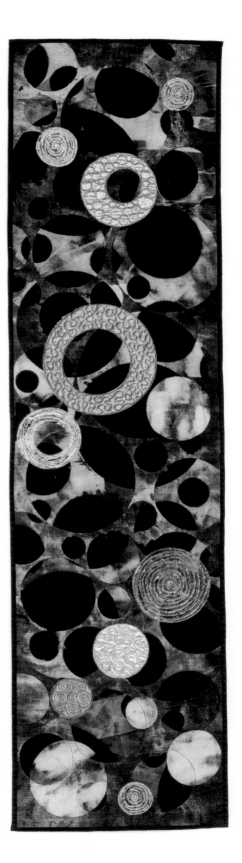

Washing out your fabric

It is advisable to wash your fabric as soon as possible. You can wash by hand or in your washing machine, at 40°C, without detergent – the water will be black! Should your fabric still smell of decolourant or bleach after washing – wash again.

Once dry, your fabric can be used like any other. Keep it whole to stitch into or cut it up and combine with other fabrics and use as appliqué.

For my series *Copperplate I, II*, and *III* I used synthetic paper lamé fabric to appliqué on top for extra 'bling'. This was stitched and then cut/burnt with a soldering iron to seal the edge. Some of the synthetic circles were further distressed with a heat gun.

Enjoy exploring my *'Life's a Bleach!'* discharging technique. I would love to see your experiments in the WOWbook members-only Facebook group.

< *Copperplate I, II* and *III* uses synthetic paper lamé fabric appliquéd on the surface for extra effect. This has been stitched and then the edges sealed using a soldering iron and distressed with a heat gun.

OLD NETS, NEW ART
Transfer dyeing with free machine embroidery

Melanie Missin

In place of net curtains you could use pieces of polyester lace fabric. As transfer dyes are used, you will need to make sure the net or lace is polyester-based for the colours of the dyes to be really deep and rich. Cotton net or lace will give you much paler shades.

In this workshop I show you how I've used some pre-loved net curtains to make a wallhanging. The techniques are very easy to learn and once the basics have been mastered, you can experiment and take the method further in your own way.

∧ The triptych shown here was made using the technique described in this workshop. Pre-loved net curtains have been transfer dyed and bonded to S80 Vilene.

MATERIALS AND EQUIPMENT

- Net curtains, with a pretty design
- Photocopy/printer paper or similar for transfer dyes
- Fusible webbing such as Misty Fuse or Fuse FX
- S80 Vilene
- Transfer dyes, paints or crayons
- Soldering iron
- Soldering iron stand – I use an upturned flowerpot
- Face mask or respirator to avoid the risk of breathing in toxic fumes
- Sewing machine set to free machine stitching
- Matching or contrasting cotton or rayon machine embroidery threads
- Heat- or air-erasable fabric pen
- Baking paper
- Iron and ironing surface
- Watercolour, silk paints, acrylic paints or Inktense blocks

> Detail of finished piece.

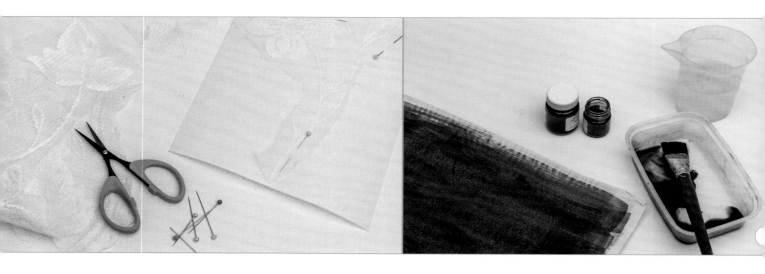

∧ Suitable motifs from net curtains have been roughly cut out, ready to use.

∧ Use transfer crayons, paints or dye powder on thin, non-absorbent paper in your colour of choice for the background piece.

Getting started

Colouring the background fabric and the motif

1. Roughly cut out the area of the net curtain motif you wish to use. I found a whole flower with some leaves attached that I thought would make a great design for my finished piece.

2. Paint one piece of the photocopy paper with transfer dye in your chosen background colour and allow to dry. For my sample I used a light turquoise.

Use a piece of baking paper on both the top and the bottom of your S80 Vilene when transferring the colour. The bottom piece will protect your ironing surface and the top one will protect your iron.

Transfer dyes

These are available as crayons, paints or dye powder (also known as disperse dye). The crayons and paints are used as they are but the dye powder is added to water, allowing you to get the exact shade of colour you require – depending upon the amount of dye powder you use.

1. Using any of the transfer mediums, draw, paint or dab using a sponge onto thin non-absorbent paper such as photocopy paper, and leave to dry.

2. Once dry, place the paper, coloured side down, onto your fabric and cover with baking paper. Set your iron to the hottest setting then slowly move the iron across the surface. This will take a few minutes. Carefully lift the edge of the paper from time to time to check how the transfer dye is working. The more you iron, the deeper the resulting colour will be. Remember to keep moving the iron slowly – if you linger in one place too long, the end result will be very patchy.

3. Cut two pieces of S80 Vilene, about 1½in (3.75cm) larger than your net curtain motif. Place baking paper on your ironing surface and lay the Vilene on top. Place the transfer-dyed paper onto the Vilene, coloured side down, and cover with a further sheet of baking paper. Now, using your iron on the hottest setting, slowly work from one side to the other. Iron the transfer-painted paper onto both pieces of your Vilene, making sure that both pieces are fully covered with colour.

4. Now paint the remaining piece of photocopy paper with the transfer dyes in the colour you have chosen for your net curtain motif. I used purple as it looks much darker than the turquoise background.

5. Place the net curtain motif face up onto one piece of the dyed Vilene (do not pin it). Place your transfer-painted paper face down on top and iron as before. Check regularly that the net curtain motif is being printed evenly.

> This is the finished motif and background piece after ironing. The second colour has transferred on top of the background colour and the motif, leaving the original colour underneath.

6. Once the colouring of the background and the motif has been completed and has dried, set your sewing machine for free machine stitching. Using a contrasting or matching cotton or rayon thread, stitch around the edges of the motif shape on the background piece, two or three times.

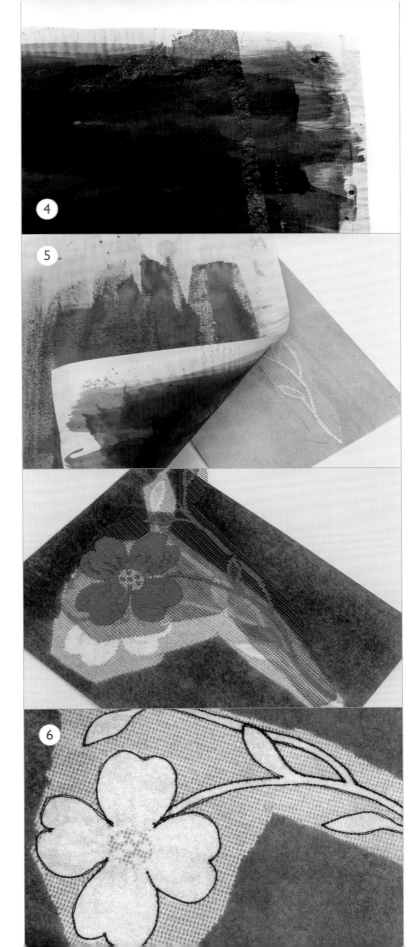

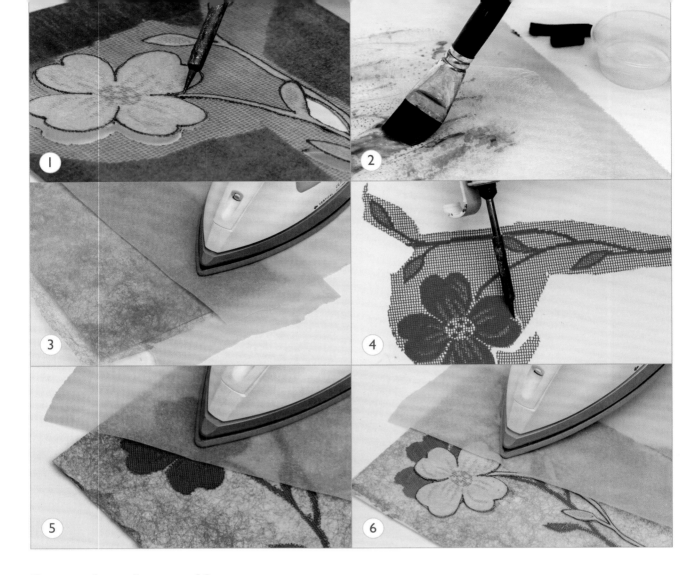

Preparing the motif

Heat the soldering iron. While it is heating and in between using it, place the soldering iron in a stand of some description to avoid any accidents. I use an upturned flowerpot; if you put some wire wool inside the pot, it will help clean the tip of the soldering iron while it is resting.

1. Use the soldering iron to cut out the coloured motif and put this to one side. Make sure you work in a well-ventilated area. I recommend that you wear a face mask or respirator when using the soldering iron, to avoid breathing in toxic fumes.

2. Paint enough fusible webbing to cover the remaining piece of coloured S80 Vilene. I used Derwent Inktense blocks. You could also try watercolours, silk paints or acrylic paints diluted with water. This will give the fusible webbing a light colour. Allow to dry completely before use.

3. Using a hot iron, fuse the webbing onto your coloured S80 Vilene background. Remember to use baking paper to protect the surface and your iron. The coloured fusible webbing gives the background a lovely textured effect.

4. Once again, use the soldering iron to cut out the flower motif from the roughly cut piece of net curtain.

5. With the fusible webbing side of the coloured background S80 Vilene facing up, place the net curtain motif slightly off centre. Iron carefully using baking paper to prevent any sticking.

6. Iron fusible webbing to the wrong side of the motif that you cut out earlier. Place the motif, fusible webbing side down, slightly to one side of the net curtain motif, to create a shadow effect.

Adding detail

1. Add extra detail to the motif using a heat- or air-erasable fabric pen. This will give you the stitching guidelines.

2. Free machine stitch your details following the marked guidelines. If you have used a heat-erasable pen, place baking paper over the piece and press with a hot iron to remove the pen marks.

3. Carefully fill in the details with watercolour paint. You could use Inktense blocks or pencils to achieve the same effect.

4. Use the side of the soldering iron to carefully burn all the way around the edges of the piece.

TIP

If you don't want to use the soldering iron you could always use a decorative machine stitch in a matching or contrasting colour to give definition to the edges.

Finishing off

1. Cut a piece of S80 Vilene 1in (2.5cm) larger
all the way around than the piece that has
been previously worked on. Transfer dye
as before in the same colour you used for
your net curtain motif. Place the motif piece
onto it centrally – this will be stitched down
securely in the next step.

2. To make the hanging tabs, transfer dye the
S80 Vilene in either a matching or contrasting
colour to the background. Cut two pieces
each 1 x 4in (2.5 x 10cm). Machine stitch or
burn the edges, as before, using the soldering
iron. Fold the tabs in half and place each one
at the top of the hanging, about 1in (2.5cm)
away from each side, making sure that the
open end is neatly tucked in between the
outer and inner piece. Machine stitch around
all sides ¼in (0.5cm) away from the motif
edge. This will also secure the tabs.

Taking it further

Why not try ...

- cutting single shapes to make hanging ornamental pieces
- using polyester or nylon lace instead of net curtain
- stitching shapes together to make a frieze of coloured motifs
- using single shapes to decorate book covers and journals
- appliquéing the coloured motifs to a background fabric before quilting.

This is a simple but very effective technique and uses materials that most of us already have in our cupboards.

< Finished piece,
Flora in Silhoue-net.

I look forward to seeing your interpretations on the WOWbook members-only Facebook group or on our blog.

PROVENÇAL LANDSCAPE
Batik on tissue

Jenny O'Leary

I've loved using batik as a technique since I was a student. I have fond memories of wax melting in a little bowl over a pan of simmering hot water on my cooker, applying it to white cotton attached to a frame and then immersing the whole fabric in a bowl of Dylon dye, leaving it for an hour, rinsing, drying then stretching it on the frame again. I would repeat this whole process using a slightly darker dye each time. It was a lengthy but exciting process.

Some years later, I discovered that painting the dyes rather than dipping them made the whole process much quicker and more accessible. I have developed a technique for combining tissue paper, bleach and ink with wax, then adding stitch to my work – either by hand or using free machine embroidery. I love the drawn quality that this adds.

I will often begin a piece of work by looking through my photographs and I also use sketchbooks for inspiration. These can take the form of a book inspired by a holiday or a visit, a particular theme, or an exploration of ideas.

> Sketchbook pages used for inspiration.

Provençal Landscape

This workshop was inspired by a visit last year to Provence. I have worked on dark brown tissue paper – the colour when bleached gives a lovely warmth to the image – but you can experiment with any colour. Before I begin the process, I often create a collage of papers.

Once you master the initial technique, I hope you will enjoy experimenting.

∧ Using my sketchbook for inspiration, the next step is to translate my ideas ready to begin a piece of new work.

> *Provençal Landscape,* finished piece.

REMEMBER ...

- Wax protects and retains colour.
- Bleach, or Milton sterilising fluid, removes the colour.
- Ink or dye adds colour.
- When you add hot wax, you are doing this because you are about to add or take away colour.
- Once waxed, the area is permanently fixed and although the wax is ironed off at the end, the surface will not take any more ink.

MATERIALS AND EQUIPMENT

- A4 size white cartridge paper, lining paper, handmade paper or watercolour paper
- A4 size coloured tissue paper – I prefer brown or black
- Glue stick
- Paintbrush
- Water pot
- White chalk
- Wax melting pot – Tixor Malam make a good one. You could use an electric frying pan or mini fryer as they have thermostats.
- Brushes for wax. I use Chinese brushes for fine lines.
- Other tools for working with wax – tjanting, pastry brush, cotton buds, comb, cardboard, etc.
- Soya wax flakes or a paraffin/beeswax mix (traditionally used for batik)
- Sterilising fluid or thin household bleach
- Small plastic travel spray
- Brush for bleach
- Drawing inks, acrylic inks or dyes. Procion dyes work well – just mix with water. I like to remove ink during the process but some acrylic inks may not work well in this way.
- Paint palette
- Soft paintbrush
- Old iron
- Newspaper

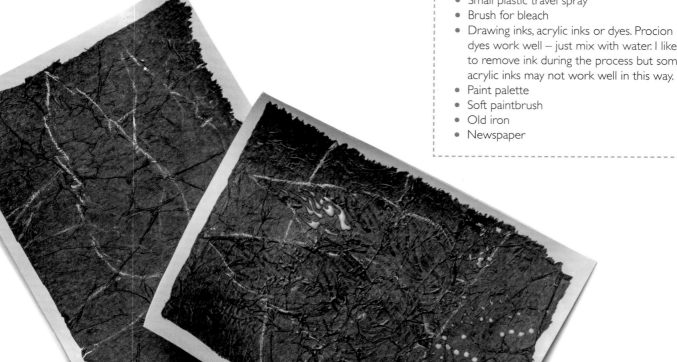

Getting started

1. Start with a piece of A4 sized white cartridge paper (you could also use lining, watercolour or handmade paper). Cut a piece of coloured tissue paper slightly smaller than your A4 paper. For this workshop, I was inspired by my trip to Provence, so I have used brown tissue paper to reflect those colours.

2. Take your piece of tissue paper and screw it up into a ball. Then completely flatten it out using the palm of your hand before gluing it to the cartridge paper. I use a glue stick to do this. Take care to cover all of the white paper with glue, as raised parts of tissue can tear easily. If you prefer, you could create an interesting torn-edged effect, as I have. To do this, paint a line of water onto the tissue paper then tear it along the wet line.

3. Draw your chosen design onto the tissue paper using white chalk as a guide to show you where to apply the wax. I have drawn a country landscape with a couple of trees for my piece. A simple design is fine.

4. Heat the wax in the wax heater. Soya wax melts at a lower temperature so as a guide, set the dial at halfway, then test. The wax shouldn't smoke but should look dark and wet when applied to your paper. Paint the wax over your chalk outlines using a paintbrush. I like to use a fine Chinese brush. The wax should be absorbed into the surface but be careful to keep a nice clean line – not too wide. Remember, you will eventually see the original colour underneath.

TIP
You could use a cold wax instead. I often use brushable wax resist which can be applied with a brush or palette knife, on stamps or through stencils.

Brushable Wax Resist
50 gm   Made in UK
Zest-it
Use as a resist for water based media.

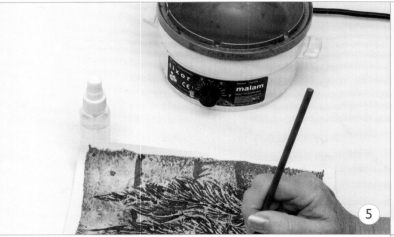

(5) (6)

5. Use different tools to create patterns and marks on your landscape. I used a brush to suggest foliage marks in the trees and a comb adds texture in the fields. Wax cools quickly, so once you remove the brush from the heater, apply it to your design, tapping your brush lightly first to lose any drips. Remember that wherever you apply wax, you are protecting the colour underneath.

TIP
Use different tools to apply the wax – a brush suggests foliage marks in trees and a comb adds texture to fields.

6. As the wax is protecting the colour, we are now ready to remove the colour from the unprotected areas. This is done with sterilising fluid – the type used for babies' bottles. You could also use thin household bleach. Dilute with approximately one-third of water and apply using a small plastic spray bottle. Spraying it on will produce a lovely speckled effect but you could also paint the fluid or bleach onto your work with a soft paintbrush.

7. Leave your piece to dry completely. Once it's dry, you could apply more wax to some areas to retain the colour of the bleached tissue. On my piece, I waxed parts of the fields.

8. Next, apply coloured drawing inks to the tissue where you have removed the colour. Brushing a little water on the surface first helps the flow of the ink and prevents it from drying too quickly. Colour can be blended on the surface. Let the ink dry completely before moving on to the next step.

9. Again, more wax can now be applied to retain areas of colour. You could add darker colours or remove colour using sterilising fluid or diluted bleach. Be aware that some acrylic inks may not work with this process. Leave your work to dry completely.

10. When your work is completely dry, you can remove the wax. To do this, place your work between two sheets of old newspaper and iron with a hot iron. To protect your iron, place baking parchment between your iron and the newspaper. Keep changing the paper to avoid putting the wax back. When there is no more wax visible on the newspaper, and your batik doesn't look shiny, it is ready.

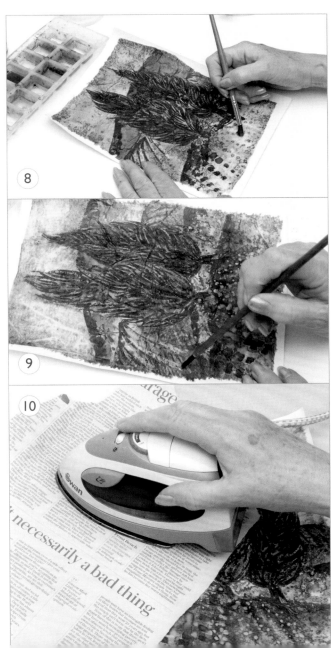

> *Provençal Landscape*, detail.

To finish

Your batik landscape is now complete.

You may wish to further enhance your batik piece with either hand stitch or using free machine embroidery. Use backing paper to support your work or, if needed, you could add an iron-on interfacing to the reverse.

To frame, I would recommend that your work is glued to a slightly thicker base, such as card, to make the piece more weighty – then mount under glass.

∧ *Light Through the Trees.*
Batik on tissue on cotton and
machine stitched. 11 x 16in
(27 x 40cm).

> *The Trees Hear Our Words,*
detail. Batik on tissue,
newspaper on canvas.
31.5 x 12in (80 x 30cm).

Taking it further

You can push this idea further in many ways. Why not try ...

- changing the format – maybe consider a panoramic viewpoint
- creating a larger piece which, when finished, you could cut into three strips vertically to create a triptych
- experimenting with different tools to create texture in the landscape
- sticking your tissue to a stretched canvas instead of plain paper at the start (use PVA glue to do this); give the canvas piece two coats of acrylic wax to make a more touchable, protected finish
- enhancing the finished piece with oil pastels, gently rubbed onto the textured surface.

THE BEAUTY OF DESTRUCTION
Maggie Grey talks to Jean Draper

Q Jean, we worked together at the Embroiderers' Guild for some time and I think it was at a time of great change for the organisation. Can you tell us something about your time as Chairman of the Guild?

A It was indeed a time of great change. Just after I became Chairman, the Arts Council announced that lottery funding was going to be made available to arts organisations, so the Guild began the long and difficult process of applying for the funding. To this end, many extra meetings were required. Once we heard that we had been awarded funding, long and intense meetings became the norm as we gradually made plans to fulfill the Arts Council's requirements so that the funding would be released in agreed stages. This work was still underway when my term of office was completed after six years. Alongside this, the normal work of the Executive Committee and the wider Guild continued. We grew and strengthened membership and one of my greatest wishes was to create firmer links between members, the Guild branches and the Guild at Hampton Court. I was with the Guild for twelve years in all, six as an Executive Committee member then six as Chairman. The hard work was worth it because of the wonderful members I met up and down the country, the experience I gained and all that I learned.

Q During your time as Chairman, you oversaw the launch of *Stitch* magazine as a sister publication to the long-standing *Embroidery*. How did this come about?

A The need for a second magazine was very carefully researched and *Stitch* was launched with the intention of attracting a readership who were perhaps more used to working from kits and needed encouragement to become more adventurous and creative in their stitching. *Stitch* became very successful from the outset.

∨ Sketchbook studies of details of rock formations in ink, wash and watercolour relating to *Tall Rock Forms* and several other works.

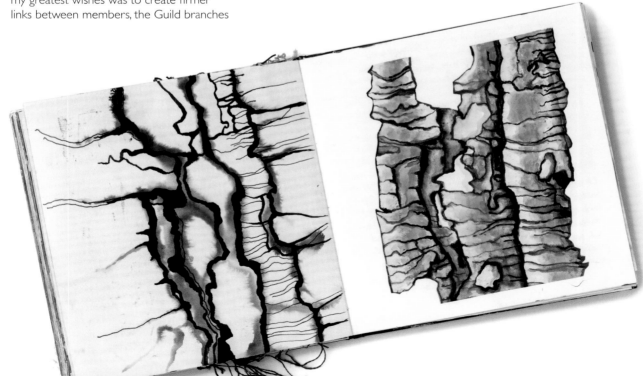

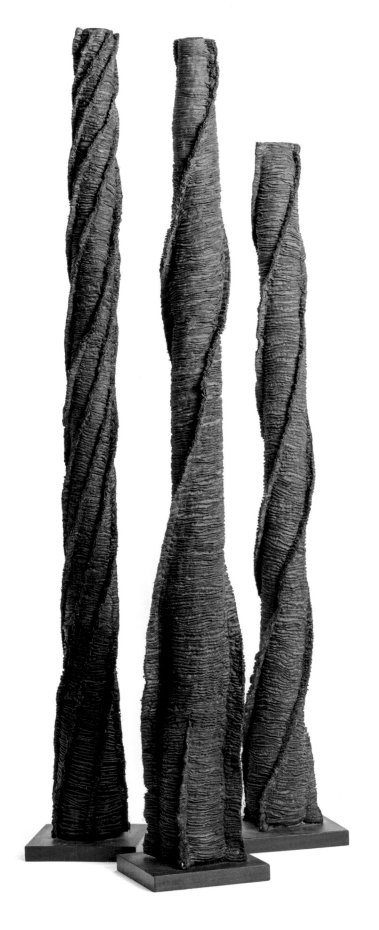

> *Tall Rock Forms.*
Left to right, height of *Forms* 42in,
41in, 39in (106cm, 105cm, 98cm).
Symbolic of monolithic rock
formations in the American south-
west, these sculptural forms are
constructed over a metal armature
and stand on slate bases. They are
hand and machine stitched on
cotton fabric, dyed and painted.

∧ *Dried Seed Pod.*
8 x 8 x 4.5in (20 x 20 x 12cm). This piece was hand stitched using fine Japanese hemp with wrapped strings and vintage millinery stamens. The work references both landscape details from the American south-west and baskets made by the indigenous people there.

< *Village Women and Children.* 10 x 6.5in (26 x 17cm). Aiming to capture the shimmering colour of the women's garments in the sun as they went about their daily tasks, scraps of bright turban cottons were applied to a background of fine indigo-dyed felt. The piece was hand stitched all over in running and other simple straight stitches using fine cotton and silk threads. The absence of outlines contributes to the effect of the glowing movement of cloth.

Q My first memory of your work is a very clear one. I had just started City & Guilds and our tutor took a coach-load of students to your exhibition in Bristol. To say that we were all overwhelmed was probably an understatement and I think that seeing your work, so early in our course, made a huge difference to the way we perceived embroidery, especially hand stitching, as an art form. I think this was quite early in your career when you were working on an Indian theme, depicting women at work. Can you give us a brief insight into the journey from this style to the beautiful austerity of your later work?

A Since the early 1970s my work has been about landscape, particularly the places I knew well that had significance for me in the UK. Often they were strongly associated with people. My early work was an expressive but more literal representation of the subject matter and, at this point, I began to develop the drawing/stitch style you mention. The exhibition you saw was in 1991. I had been a member of the 62 Group since about 1976, regularly exhibiting with them.

As I had been teaching full-time in schools, colleges and, latterly, at the University of Wolverhampton, I had done very little

freelance work so, at that stage, I was not too well known. By 1991, I had taken early retirement from my post as Senior Lecturer and was more 'out and about' in the textile world. The work in the Bristol exhibition was strongly influenced by my second textile study trip to India when I was intent on exploring the rich use of colour and pattern seen there, but it was still all about 'place', the architecture, villages, people and animals that I had observed and drawn there. During my three study trips to India, I learned a great deal about the village women, their textiles and their direct, deceptively simple, ways of stitching using the most basic of materials. This has been a huge and continuing influence.

Sometime later, following many visits to the American south-west (when I discovered the beauty of the stark desert landscapes), I worked on expressing my reactions to these very different places, which enabled me to encompass some of the history of the area and the people who had inhabited and worked that land. In many of the pieces I made at that time, I concentrated on details of the land, such as rock and earth surfaces, unusual plant forms, dried grasses and thorns. Studying these led to my first experiments with three-dimensional work.

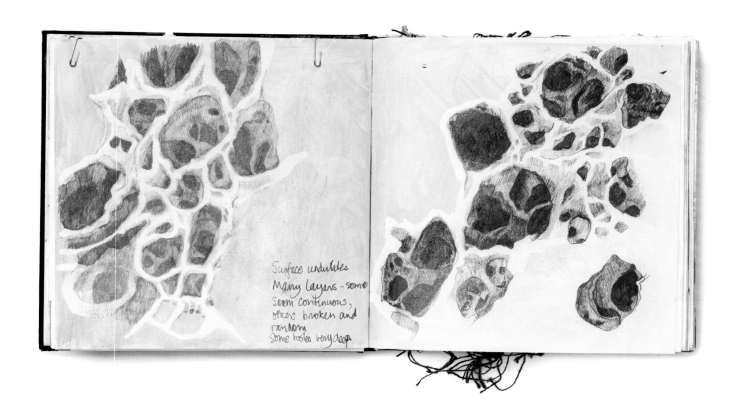

Surface undulates
Many Layers – some
seam continuous,
others broken and
random
Some holes very deep

∧ Two of many sketchbook studies, in pencil and gouache, of areas of an eroded cliff face. These were made before undertaking the piece called *Tafoni*, shown on page 60.

Q I know that you have always advocated drawing and that you focused on that in your National Diploma in Design. I came into stitch through drawing and still have phases where I forsake the needle for the pencil. Do you think drawing is an essential part of textile art and what advice would you have for those who shy away from it? In other words, what do you think might be a good starting point for a beginner?

A My training was four years in art college where drawing, painting and design were emphasised throughout. The first two years were a general art course leading to an intermediate examination and my final two years led to the National Diploma in Design; I specialised in Dress Design and Hand Embroidery (in those days a distinction was made between hand and machine embroidery). Finally, a year at London University Institute of Education enabled me to gain my teaching degree equivalent (ATC).

I believe drawing to be essential in making original, personal work. For me, drawing is a way of looking and, through looking hard, beginning to understand, know and record the world around me. This applies especially to subject matter that interests me most, or newly discovered places and things.

Drawing is sometimes described as 80% looking and 20% making marks on paper. Immediately on beginning to draw, personal interpretation of the subject led on to ideas for translation into stitch. My sketchbooks are personal and very important to me, containing, as well as drawings, jotted notes, maybe suggestions for further investigations and ideas for stitching. My sketchbook drawings are not always 'finished' or very polished, but instead they provide information for my work about places I have visited and interesting things seen. Sometimes the drawings are very swift – just visual reminders, with a few added notes.

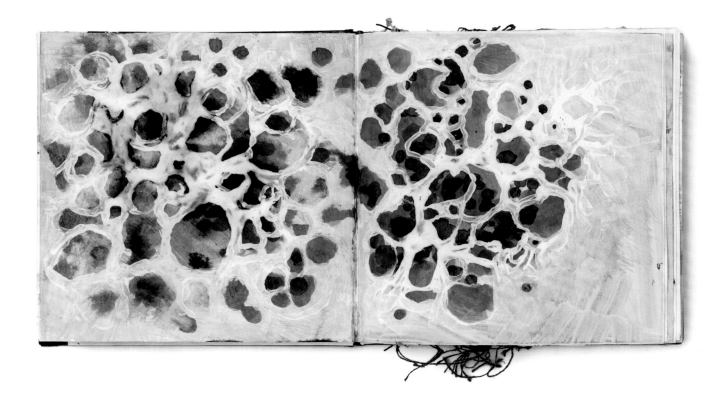

Over the years I have developed a preferred style of drawing in which layers of bold directional mark-making resemble and relate to the way I like to use stitches. These, in turn, are often simple and straight, but of different sizes and weights and in varying threads. I have often described this process as drawing how I stitch and stitching how I draw. My stitching has always been multi-layered and very labour intensive. I draw *in situ* whether outdoors or in museums (see subject matter below). Sometimes I take photographs for reference for use in my studio, but never in order to copy as a finished textile design. I never draw or paint a finished design and then stitch it, but tend to make small rough sketch layouts, using as reference the various drawings I have already made.

Drawing is an essential part of my textile practice but others might think and work differently, perhaps using a computer or tracing paper to generate designs. I love different drawing materials in my hands and the direct feeling of contact with paper.

Many people shy away from drawing. Perhaps they have been told in school that they cannot draw, maybe even had their efforts ridiculed. I believe everyone can draw, not necessarily to become a great artist, but to make honest representations, perhaps diagrammatic ones, by looking, understanding and becoming absorbed in things that interest them. Rather than trying to draw a whole object in a totally literal manner, it is often helpful to zone in on one aspect or detail that particularly appeals, such as pattern, texture, edges, lines within etc. Careful studies of these can often suggest stitch interpretations. The important thing to remember is that the drawings made are for your personal information and do not have to make sense, or be shown to anyone else for their approval.

∧ Other sketchbook studies of 'holey' subjects inspired further work.

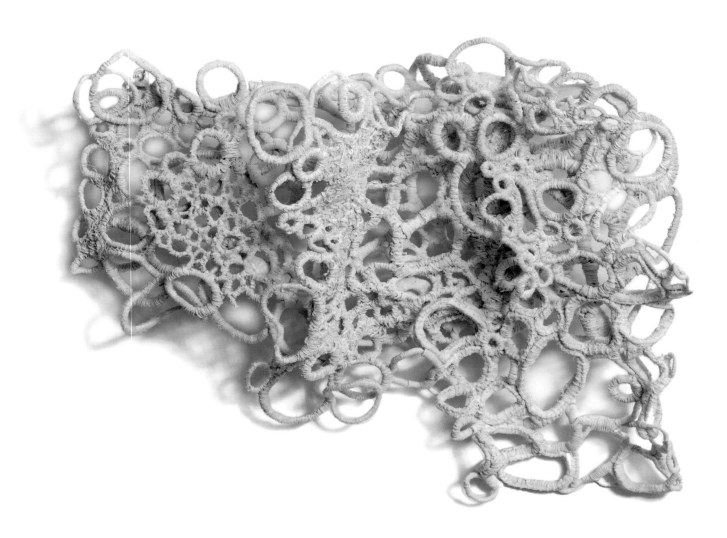

∧ *Tafoni.* 17 × 20 × 6.5in (43 × 50 × 17cm). This name is derived from the geological term for the eroded cliff seen at Elgol on the Isle of Skye. The high-relief wall piece was constructed from many wrapped rings of different sizes. Materials used: hemp and cotton threads, wire and paint.

< Sketchbook studies in pencil and gouache of dried saguaro cactus, showing shapes and connectedness of holes.

DRIED SAGUARD CACTUS

∧ *Small Dried Seed Pods.*
4 x 3 x 3in (10 x 8 x 8cm)
and 4.5 x 2.5 x 2.5in
(11 x 7 x 7cm).
Hand stitched over a
mould (later removed)
in natural hemp with
added paint. Threads
under tension were firmly
wrapped to create a
rigid structure.

> Sketchbook pages showing
experimental images and
rough notes for possible
stitch interpretations.
Pencil, paint and soft pastel.

The sketchbook notes read:
- Sculptural wallpieces
- Dense, heavy outsides,
- Fragile centres
- Must create tension
1. Could be black/grey
2. Could have some colour
3. Could be highly coloured
- Shadows

*Possible working with
wrapped curly-willow.*

< *Sketchbook.* Watercolour study of cracks and crevices in the desert landscape in which the variation and direction of line is all-important. On the right-hand page of the sketchbook, a simplified tonal analysis, drawn in pencil, of the main vertical line.

Q You are a member of two prestigious exhibiting groups: The 62 Group and the Textile Study Group (TSG). Do you find the pressure to finish work for exhibitions daunting or does the need to fulfill the brief in a set timescale spur you on to examine differing methods of production and stretch you as an artist? How do the two groups differ?

A I have been a member of the two groups for a long time: The 62 Group since the mid-1970s and the TSG (formerly called the Practical Study Group) since the late 1980s. The groups are quite different, but nonetheless both very professional in every aspect of their aims and the way they are run.

The 62 Group has a rigorous selective approach to initial membership and to each exhibition. Selection for both is carried out by a changing committee formed of several members. If a member fails to submit work for three consecutive exhibitions, or gets work rejected three times in a row, membership is lost. Communication is by a twice-yearly Newsletter and the AGM is held each December. The emphasis in this group is on work for exhibitions.

The TSG began primarily as a group of embroidery teachers who wanted to promote good teaching. The exhibitions they held every so often were, I think, intended to inspire people with more innovative forms of embroidery, as were the books written jointly by the group. Many members were teachers

of City & Guilds courses who were also, individually, authors of embroidery and textile books. We meet twice yearly for residential Continuing Professional Development weekends when we work intensively with different tutors. Our AGM, which we are required to attend, is held on one of these weekends.

There is a selection process for joining the TSG, but we keep the group number to 25, because we value relationships within the group, enjoying working together in one large room with one tutor. For the exhibitions there is usually no selection procedure but, in a recent one (and the upcoming one next year), we have had the advice of a Curator. Every five years, members' work is reviewed by an appointed outside person; we are individually interviewed and receive written comments. Currently, the TSG is working on an exhibition and book called *Insights* (to be published in 2020) in which each member will write a chapter detailing individual working processes and development. Proposals for themes and text have been submitted and approved by the editors and the curator.

I am also part of another exhibiting group that is very important to me. The Broadway Group is made up of four dedicated textile artists with very different professional backgrounds and skills who meet regularly to discuss and critique our work. Although we do this with care and respect and are very supportive of each other, we are honest and serious in what we say and suggest. I find this very refreshing and stimulating.

> *Small Burned Plant Form.* 8 x 8 x 7in (20 x 20 x 18cm). This piece was inspired by the many small clumps of burnt and scorched bushes and sage brush that are left after fires have swept the land in the American south-west. The landscape then appeared to be full of black dots. It was made from sticks and paper threads on a raised base.

> Jean's sketchbook pages (right) lead on to the resolved work shown above.

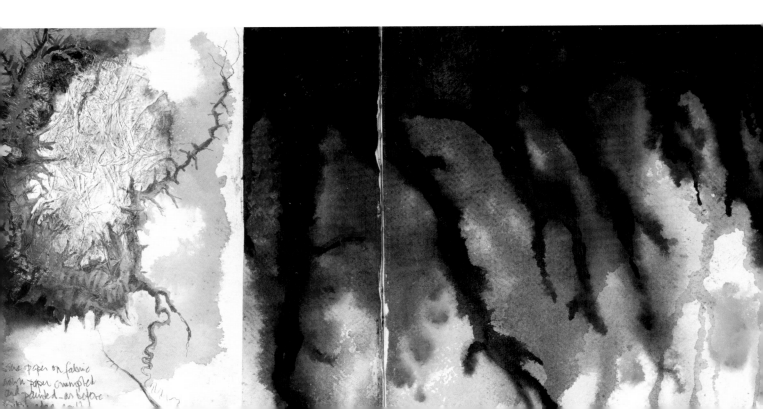

Q While on the subject of showing work, I really have to make reference to the Textile Study Group's Dis/*rupt* exhibition in 2017–18 which was curated by Dr Melanie Miller, a well-respected figure in the textile world. The concept was based on the premise that in so many areas of the world, the only certainty is chaos. It's hard not to agree when considering issues of climate, conflict and political issues at home and worldwide. Clive and I reviewed this exhibition for the WOWbook website and our visit took place at the tail-end of a relaxing weekend away – maybe that intensified the effect that this soul-searing drama of an exhibition had on us. The artists' reaction to the theme was amazing. It was, I think, intended to shock people out of complacency and it certainly succeeded in that. How did you all come up with the theme and did it affect the artists as much as it did the viewers?

A Dis/*rupt* was organised by an exhibition sub-committee which came up with the title that the whole group then agreed. The concept was that members should willingly challenge (or disrupt) their thinking and working practice, to work outside their 'comfort zone' and make work on one of the three suggested themes: Conflict, the Environment, or Technology. I'm not aware that the intention was to shock viewers of the exhibition but, rather, for TSG members to be challenged to make different and meaningful work.

> *Forbidden*.
Approximately 35 x 71in (90 x 180cm). An installation of burnt books made in response to the brief of 'Conflict' for the Textile Study Group's Dis/*rupt* exhibition. Built around the notion that books can be regarded as dangerous, even threatening, by some people and groups, Jean decided to attempt to comment on the lack of understanding and discrimination seen and heard everywhere. Old books, donated by friends and purchased from charity shops, were subjected to various kinds of abuse with wrapped and knotted wire, rags, chains and nails, then burnt so that they and their contents were destroyed. The aim was to create a stark piece of work to provoke thoughts about anger and mindless vandalism.

Perhaps unsettled at the beginning of the project, most of us were deeply affected by our chosen subject matter as research and work progressed. When the exhibition opened, it was refreshing and satisfying to see the different approaches and the recognition that stitched textiles don't necessarily have to be 'pretty' and polite, but can be expressive and sometimes very raw visually and emotionally. Perhaps the acceptance of mixed media alongside our usual materials has added to the scope of possibilities although, of course, women in the past have often used their stitching as a vehicle for political and/or subversive statements.

During the times that I stewarded the exhibition, I was struck by viewers' responses. Perhaps after their initial surprise in some cases, I saw people very engaged with the work, reading the explanations and entering into discussion with their companions and those of us who were around. I understand from other members that this occurred throughout the duration of the exhibition.

Q We talked about it all the way home and for weeks afterwards. The review I wrote for WOW resulted in the most correspondence we've ever received on a single topic: Siân Martin's tale of the immigrant lad, kissing his mother and running away, Dorothy Tucker's washing lines (before and after a village was attacked) and, of course, your unforgettable installation of burnt books.

I don't think that we were the only people affected in this way. Clive said it was the one of the best exhibitions he has ever seen and, as a compulsive reader, he was much affected by your burnt book exhibit, *Forbidden*. Can you tell us more about that, please?

A My installation *Forbidden* was a natural progression from a group of small burnt books I had made a few years ago. I had witnessed and was deeply affected by the immediate aftermath of a devastating forest fire in Arizona where many thousands of mostly pine trees had been burnt. Later, in thinking how I might use some of this imagery in my work, I realised that many of these trees would probably have been used for making paper and then books. So began my small burnt book series, some of which had spiky edges like some of the broken trees I had seen. The notion of books that cannot be read because they have thorns and spikes on them, led to the overall title *Books Can Be Dangerous*, meaning both physically dangerous as well as the content being, in some people's eyes, dangerous and seditious too. One or two of this series had been made from actual burnt paperback books, others constructed from painted and burnt handmade paper.

∨ *Forbidden*, detail. Books were 'gagged' with wrapping and abused with nails, barbed and other wire; they were then burnt. They can no longer be read.

For the Dis/rupt sub-category 'Conflict', I wanted to reflect and comment on the upsetting cruelty, lack of understanding and discrimination that we see around us constantly in all levels of society and throughout the world. When one nation or race dominates or oppresses another, usually the culture and religion of the weaker people are crushed and destroyed. Many instances of this exist both historically and presently throughout the world. In making *Forbidden* I used the destruction of books to symbolise the control and annihilation of the culture and traditions of less powerful or conquered people.

The challenge for me was on several levels: first, how to make a strong, raw political and unapologetic statement without slogans or superficiality; then, wondering if I could handle the size of the piece. Lastly, and the most difficult, was the actual burning and brutalising of the books, which I found emotionally very difficult. Some of the methods used to prevent the books being opened and read were nailing, stitching and tying, using barbed and other wires to bind around the books, and chains and locks to close them.

∧ *Forbidden*, detail.

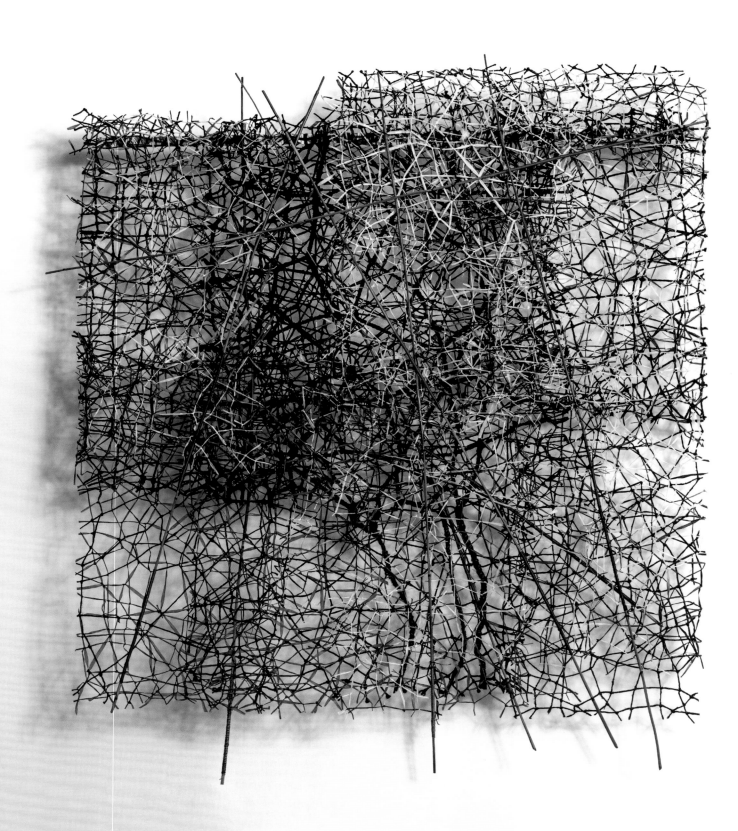

> *Excluded.* 17 x 15in (43 x 38cm). This was constructed in the same way as *Restricted Access* (below), but with the addition of relevant words embedded in the thread layers. Both of these are very recent pieces. They relied on tension to create the self-supporting structure without the need for a background fabric.

< *Restricted Access.* 30 x 26in (75 x 65cm). Having in mind dense undergrowth and impenetrable thorny plants seen growing in difficult-to-access places, Jean made this piece, and *Excluded* (see above). Although the starting point was landscape details, they reference the social injustice that is seen everywhere. The method is based on large-scale knotted needlelace fillings making many layers of open meshes, using Japanese paper threads, conventional embroidery threads, wrapped wire and fine sticks.

Q As always, the final question must be about your current work. Are you continuing the theme of the beauty of destruction, burning and barren landscapes? What's next on your horizon?

A As ever, my work is very labour intensive as the directional repetitive gestures I employ in my hand stitching are an important part of my working process. I continue to look to landscape for starting points and am using stylised details of dense plant forms, thorny bushes etc. for initial visual impact. However, as I am constantly affected by what I see, hear and read about disturbing current issues of concern, I still want to comment on some of these themes in my work. I aim therefore to give thought-provoking titles to suggest hidden meanings to the pieces. An example of this is the illustrated work called *Restricted Access* based on criss-crossing stems and dried grasses, the many layers of which would be physically difficult to penetrate, but also intended to imply unfair restrictions imposed on some people through various forms of discrimination. Using similar themes, I am also continuing to develop some new sculptural book forms.

∨ Leaf cube (leaf, wool, hand stitch in silk thread). Stone with wrapping and hand stitch in linen; cordage ball made with gathered plant material.

Alice Fox

I've always been fascinated by the natural world and interacting creatively with what I find there. I'm committed to an environmentally low-impact approach to making, relishing the challenge of working within a set of self-imposed parameters and aiming to be as self-sufficient in materials as possible. Embracing serendipity and recognising beauty and complexity in the everyday, I use found objects and gathered materials. I take an experimental approach in learning about possibilities to exploit these objects and materials for making marks, stains, structures and surfaces.

> Looped paper vessel with Severn estuary mud; stitched limpet shell with cotton/silk thread.

My first degree in physical geography and subsequent early career in nature conservation instilled in me an appreciation for natural landforms and processes. This experience certainly underpins the way I work now as an artist. I undertook a degree in textiles as a mature student, so my understanding of textile techniques is key to my practice. However, the objects and surfaces that I make are far from conventional. I draw techniques from other disciplines including basketry and printmaking. I'm fundamentally interested in the materiality of the things available to me locally and enjoy learning about a material through working with it.

> *Tide Line*, detail, 2013. Found rusty objects with weave in cotton and rust staining.

I am a member of the Textile Study Group, through which I exhibit, teach and learn. I have also shown work in a variety of solo and group exhibitions. Making work for an exhibition is a good way of focusing one's energies, but sharing knowledge through writing, teaching and talks is also rewarding. I have enjoyed landscape-based and library-based residencies: seemingly different contexts, but my approach is always materials- and objects-centred. During a project in Newcastle City Library, I made *Unknown Book*, exploring the qualities of different papers available, staining, stitching and binding to make a work that referenced a particular book in the collection.

I recently finished an MA in Creative Practice. My allotment plot formed the focus of my practice-based research, through which I explored ideas of self-sufficiency and ways to record the plot through the cycle of seasons. I grew my own flax, which I processed and spun into linen fibre; I gathered plant material for ink-making, trying out all sorts of possibilities; I explored the different manufactured materials on the site (wood, plastic, paper, cloth, ceramic – sometimes drawing these using my homemade inks); I started to use different plant fibres to make cordage and then develop three-dimensional structures. Although I have completed the course, I've only just begun to understand the potential of what is available to me on the plot. There is much more yet to explore.

Website: **www.alicefox.co.uk**

∧ *Unknown Book*, 2017.
14 × 11 × 2.75in
(35 × 28 × 7cm). Paper, linen, acrylic, acetate, natural dyes, cyanotype, print, gold leaf. One of six panels.

< Individual components of *Unknown Book*, 2017. Paper, linen, natural dyes, cyanotype.

Holly Hart

I am an illustrator, maker and textile artist from Pembrokeshire, south-west Wales. I studied at Pembrokeshire College and Coleg Sir Gar in Carmarthen, gaining a BA in Design Studies.

After graduating I was chosen by the Embroiderers' Guild to be a part of their Graduate Showcase, where I was able to exhibit my work at the London and Harrogate Knitting & Stitching Shows. During the same year I exhibited as part of the new licentiate group with the Society of Designer Craftsmen at the Mall Galleries in London. It's a brilliant opportunity to show work around the country and meet like-minded people. Taking part in exhibitions and shows is something I will never tire of.

My background is a mixture of fine art and textiles, which I think shows in my work. This ranges from large paintings to delicate paper and fabric nature-inspired scenes, occasionally encased inside glass bell jars. I thoroughly enjoy working with a variety of materials, such as acrylic paints, recycled fabric, metallic threads and inks. For me, my sewing machine is another drawing tool. I was introduced to machine embroidery in college and instantly fell in love with this technique.

I gather my inspiration from the natural world, which never fails to impress me. My love for wildlife stems from a strong interest which started as a child; I'm grateful to my late granddad for influencing this love. Some of my earliest memories are of walks down the lane

∧ Sketchbook page. Collection of old stamps alongside my sketch of a bullfinch.

> Sketchbook page. A small portion of my bird feather collection, all found on the ground. As well as a feather collection, I also collect animal skulls (all ethically sourced).

outside my grandparents' house, eating wild strawberries. The hedgerows seemed huge back then, towering over me, full of life. British flora and fauna are my main subjects and I get many ideas from visitors to my garden and in the countryside around me. I'm blessed to live in such a beautiful part of the country.

Another of my interests is collecting vintage wildlife books. Every antiques or charity shop I visit, I cannot resist a rummage in their books section to see if I can add to my collection. There is something in the old colour illustrations that grabs me. I love how the animals in the books are often drawn in their own scene, rather than standing on their own. I enjoy drawing all creatures, from the large to the small, bringing to people's attention the creatures that are sometimes overlooked. Ornithology fascinates me – I'm a keen birder, and perhaps this is why my most frequently drawn subjects are birds. Living in Pembrokeshire, I have a wide variety of birds to choose from. Often pieces are made in celebration after a first sighting of a particular animal. I want to capture their characters in my pieces, their movement in flight, and simply to bring them to life. I believe it is important to celebrate our wildlife, in a climate where many species are in decline. Now is the time to educate people about our wildlife. If we do not know what beauty lies around us, how can we protect it and save it from disappearing for good?

Website: **www.hollyhartart.com**

∧ *Red squirrel.* Ink on calico framed in a secondhand brass frame. I love his little fluffy ears and paws.

Jenny O'Leary

Having always loved drawing and making things as a child, I began my career in art by taking a Foundation Art course, followed by a BA in Ceramics and an Art Teachers' Diploma, studying Photography and Printmaking. There was a mixed-media element to parts of the ceramics course, so my love of textiles was allowed to continue. I taught ceramics for four years and, when taking up my next teaching post, was asked to teach some textiles. My own work slowly began to develop as a result. Batik had become a real passion, along with free machine embroidery.

In 2005 I gave up my teaching post to set up my own business with my husband, running textile art courses in the UK and France. We did this successfully for five years, until my husband passed away suddenly. As a result, I stopped teaching in France and gradually built up my career at home.

Batik continues to be my main inspiration — on tissue, paper and fabric. Batik on tissue became the main focus of my work. I love the way it pushes me to search for new ways of working and developing my ideas.

I am inspired by landscape, and living in the beautiful county of Shropshire on the borders of Wales I don't have to travel far to take photographs and sketch. Rolling hills, ploughed fields and trees through the seasons have always featured in my work. Train journeys have inspired panoramic viewpoints, allowing time to look and think, attempt photographs — at speed! — and then develop them into my work. I began to include text in my work to give it a narrative. A favourite workshop of mine is batik inspired by the work of the artist John Piper.

I've always loved his work and through developing this workshop, I started using oil pastels to create resists as well as hot wax, either as rubbings or as a drawn element. Architecture as subject matter had been something I would usually avoid but again, this workshop has opened up new areas of thought.

I have recently been exploring resists in their many forms, not just hot wax but also candles, brushable wax resist, oil pastels, stencils and acrylic paint, singly and in combination. This has mainly been through sketchbook development but I'm now sharing these ideas through workshops. I love the way ideas put forward in workshops are then developed and taken in new directions by my students. The process of teaching adults is exciting for me, and I learn from my students as they do from me.

I teach workshops all around the UK, together with talks and demonstrations to Embroiderers' Guild and textile groups, and exhibit and sell my work. I regularly run workshops at the Oxford Summer School, Westhope College and at The Willow Gallery in Shropshire, where I live. I also teach in schools, both at primary and secondary level. I am a member of The Batik Guild, The Embroiderers' Guild and The Shropshire Guild of Contemporary Craft.

Website: **www.jennyolearytextiles. wordpress.com**

∧ *Olive Tree* (top left). 11.5 x 9.5in (29 x 24cm). Batik on tissue.

∧ *Broken Leaves* (top right). 7.5 x 7.5in (19 x 19cm). Batik on tissue, graphite, hand and machine stitch.

< *The Trees Hear Our Words*. 12 x 32in (30 x 80cm). Batik on tissue, newspaper on canvas.

Mary McIntosh

Originally from the north-east of England, I have moved steadily down the country and now live on the Suffolk/Essex border. My first career as a bookseller lasted 28 years and it was only from 2011, on completing my City & Guilds Diploma in Patchwork and Quilting, that I combined my hobby with my job and started a second career as a textile artist and tutor. I now work as principal tutor for Creative Stitch based in East Anglia, and offer talks and workshops throughout the UK. I'm a member of the exhibiting group Out of the Fold.

Until recently I would have described my working practice as technique-based in that I find a technique I like and then explore the different ways in which it can be developed. My exhibition pieces often start as samplers for teaching and then grow into larger pieces of work. This is how my 'Life's a Bleach!' series began. I started by using Jacquard Decolourant, applying bleach and then trying out ways of using different pigment-based products to add colour in, as well as taking it out – all using black fabric to achieve the most dramatic results. The addition of metallic fabrics as appliqué seemed to work well. This sojourn to the 'dark side' lasted several years and became a bit of an obsession.

More recently, however, my work has moved away from the dark and I am now exploring ways of adding more colour. I begin using white fabric, stitching over it using white cotton thread, and then painting, dyeing, over-dyeing and finally discharging. My 'Out of the North East' series was inspired by my Northumbrian background and, in particular, my thrifty granny, who made clippie mats (rag rugs) from donated old clothes. My version of these mats start as recycled calico and use stitched and cut buttonholes which are threaded through with strips of dyed fabric – the background is still discharged as I haven't weaned myself away from this technique entirely! I have also explored 'proggie' – the other mat-making technique – which involves pulling shorter strips of fabric through to create a lovely soft, textured rug.

I'm currently working on a new series of work inspired by the weaving industry. I was born in Jedburgh in the Scottish borders, the heart of a wool-weaving area. When I was first married with a young family, we lived in the Pennines in a former cotton-weaving town, and I now live in Sudbury, Suffolk, which still weaves 95% of the silk in the country. My next project, 'Wool – Cotton – Silk', is a series of work inspired by this great industrial past and my personal journey from north to south. My early samples are being worked as long narrow pieces which fit onto reels from one of the local Sudbury mills.

Websites: *www.marymcintosh.co.uk* and *thecopperqueen.blogspot.com*

< Long narrow pieces inspired by the weaving industry and worked onto reels from the silk mills.

> *Out of the North East – Hookie*. One of a series inspired by Northumbrian mat-making.

> *Out of the North East – Proggie* (far right).

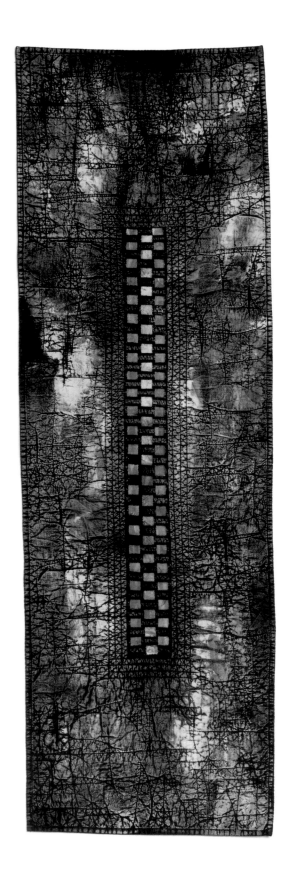
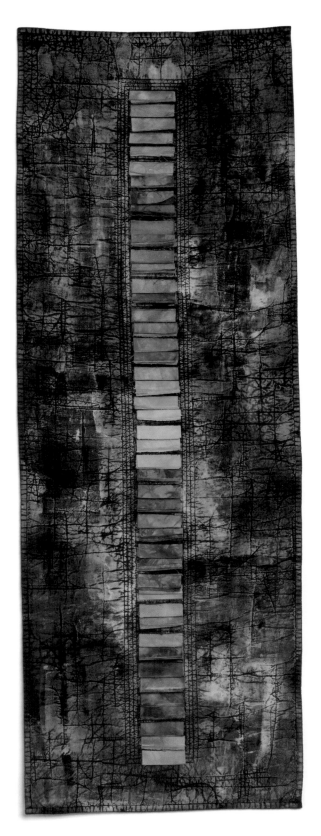

Melanie Missin

My journey in textiles came about originally from my wonderful and extremely talented mother. In my early years, mum taught me how to do many different crafts, from embroidery to macramé, beadwork to tapestry, and much more. Mum was, and still is, my inspiration.

I originate from Cornwall (my mum and family still live there) and moved up to Cambridgeshire when I was eighteen. It wasn't until I had my two boys that I delved back into stitching, beading, knitting and crochet.

In 2006, I decided that I wanted to learn how to do patchwork so I made some panels but didn't know how to piece them together. I visited mum and asked her to teach me and the rest, as they say, is history. I have never looked back. Every time I visited mum, she would have a new project for me to learn and I soaked it all up ... I was hooked!

In 2007, I started my own little patchwork group. We still meet most Thursdays and have all become firm friends but it was not until I

met Yvonne Brown and attended some of her workshops that I finally knew where I wanted to go in the textile world. Yvonne taught me so much in advanced textiles, from using a soldering iron to learning how to free machine stitch. She opened new doors and I aspire to be like her one day and share my knowledge as she does.

Yvonne has had her own stand at the Festival of Quilts for many years and I said to her that one day I would like to be where she was standing. Last year, I had my first stand at the Festival of Quilts. One achievement met.

The wonderful Mary McIntosh did a talk on City & Guilds textiles and told us how it had changed her life. In 2015, I signed up to do my City & Guilds course with her and as a result of her teaching and guidance, I have achieved work of which I am very proud, including pieces that are now touring America. I graduated in 2017.

Another amazing textile artist, Jacquie Harvey, has become my mentor (I'm not sure if she knows that!). Jacquie has helped boost my

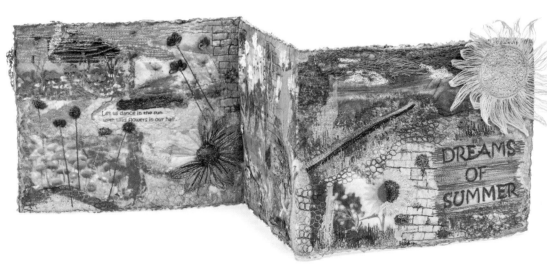

confidence by sending pieces of my work off to be included in magazines, but mostly by just being there and giving me much needed advice and encouragement.

In 2016, I opened my own studio where I teach workshops and classes. Most of my work is based on the natural world – insects, plants and colour.

I have been invited to teach at different groups around the country and have even ventured to Ireland, which was fabulous. I was recently invited to host a Colouricious holiday in Jaipur, India, in October 2019, which was a dream come true!

Website: *www.mellymadedesigns.com*

∧ *My Book of Favourite Things – Insects and Dreaming of Summer Booklet.* Both of these books were made using a medium-weight, sew-in Vilene (M12). I used quite a few different techniques to create them: tea-dyeing, painting Fuse-a-web, Tyvek and FuseFX. I printed photos and text onto the Vilene and used water-soluble film to make my 3D flowers and insects. I finished the pieces using free machine stitching.